Father BROWNE'S AUSTRALIA

Overleaf: Father Browne's first view of the Australian coast over 'the Rip' at Melbourne (April 1924)

Father BROWNE'S

AUSTRALIA

E. E. O'DONNELL S.J.

WOLFHOUND PRESS

First paperback edition 1999

First published in hardback 1995 by
Wolfhound Press Ltd
68 Mountjoy Square
Dublin 1

Father Browne prints are available from Davison and Associates, 69b Heather Road, Sandyford Industrial Estate, Dublin 18.

British Library Cataloguing in Publication Data

Father Browne's Australia: Photographs from the Francis Browne SJ Collection I. O'Donnell, E.E.
779.092

ISBN 0 86327 713 6

Typesetting: Wolfhound Press
Book design: Jan de Fouw
Cover design: Slick Fish
Cover photograph: Father Browne: Children of the Darling Downs (see page 99)
Prints: Davison & Associates
Duotone Separations: Typeform Ltd, Dublin
Printed in Ireland by Betaprint International Ltd

By the same author:

FATHER BROWNE'S AUSTRALIA
443 9 hb £19.99

FATHER BROWNE'S ENGLAND
490 0 hb £25.00

FATHER BROWNE'S CORK
489 7 hb £19.99

FATHER BROWNE'S DUBLIN
366 1 pb £19.99

FATHER BROWNE: A LIFE IN PICTURES
436 6 pb £9.99
459 5 hb £18

IMAGES OF ARAN 1925 & 1938
599 0 pb £9.99

POSTCARDS FROM THE TITANIC
696 2 pb £5.99

THE GENIUS OF FATHER BROWNE
265 7 hb £19.95

FATHER BROWNE'S IRELAND
200 2 hb £19.95

FATHER BROWNE'S TITANIC ALBUM
598 2 hb £20

errata

Page 47 For 'Children on Narrabeen Beach, now a built-up resort north of Sydney' read 'Children on Palm Beach, looking south from Barrenjoey'.

Page 49 For 'from that nearby town of Cronulla to the coast at la Peruse' read 'from that seaside town to Sutherland via Miranda'.

Page 77 For 'crossing the Paramatta River' read 'crossing the Hawkesbury River'.

Page 87 For 'Mudgee' read 'Nudgee'.

Page 95 For 'Toowoong' read 'Toowong'.

5 4 3 2 1

CONTENTS

INTRODUCTION by E. E. O'Donnell

AUSTRALIA 1924-25 by David Day

PHOTOGRAPHS by Father Browne

INTRODUCTION

When an Irish Jesuit priest died in 1960, few would have thought that his name would become famous thirty years later. Even among his Jesuit confreres, few remembered that away back in 1927 Frank Browne had put Ireland on the photographic map of the world. For over a quarter of a century his 42,000 negatives, taken in thirty different countries, lay untouched in a basement archive. All neatly dated and captioned, the negatives recorded a bygone era and the quality of the photography was special. The pictures covered a period of nearly sixty years (1897 to 1957), two of which were spent in Australia. The selection presented in this book, therefore, show some of the early work of a man who is quickly becoming recognised as a photographic genius.

Francis Mary Hegarty Browne was born in Cork City, Ireland, in 1880. He came from a prominent family of that city, his grandfather being Lord Mayor of Cork and his uncle being Bishop of the neighbouring diocese of Cloyne. In 1897, when he had completed his secondary schooling in Dublin, Frank went on a Grand Tour of Europe with his brother and his camera. Little did he think that these first snap-shots would be the opening salvo in a fusillade of photography that would still be reverberating nearly a century later.

On his return to Ireland, in September 1897, he joined the Jesuits. His two years in the novitiate near Tullamore were followed by three years at the Royal University in Dublin. This was the University College founded by Cardinal Newman where Fr Gerard Manley Hopkins SJ had been Professor of Greek until his death in 1889. Frank studied Greek there, as well as Latin and English. It is interesting to note that another Old Belvederian, James Joyce, was a strict contemporary for these three university years. Since Jesuit students were still not allowed to have cameras, however, we have no Browne portrait of the writer as a young man.

Joyce and Browne had much in common: both of their fathers came from Cork and both families originally came from Galway. The Brownes and the Joyces were numbered among the ancient tribes of that city. James and Frank had both been to school at Belvedere and both were given to philosophical speculation. Whereas James was just out of school and of an introverted disposition, Frank was twenty-two years old in 1902 and tended to be more of an extrovert. 'Mr Browne, the Jesuit' features (favourably!) in the pages of *Finnegans Wake*. Indeed the juxtaposition of the names Browne and Nolan in that book — besides alluding to the Dublin publishers of that name, to the philosopher, Bruno of Nola, etc. — might well refer to Frank Browne and a Jesuit contemporary of his, T.V. Nolan.

Joyce, too, was interested in photography and was soon to develop an interest in cinematography. He opened Dublin's first cinema, The Volta, on Mary Street, in 1909.

Although not as strict as the régime in the novitiate, the Jesuit Junior's life was still organised along fairly rigid lines. Rising at 5.55 a.m., the hour's meditation was still done before breakfast and the examination of conscience was done twice daily as in the noviceship. Then the Juniors would attend their university lectures next door but they were not allowed to fraternise with the lay-students there. Nor were they permitted to take part in university games. Instead, they played soccer against the Jesuit 'theologians' at Milltown Park on Saturday afternoons.

While Joyce and his medical student friends were men about town, the Jesuit students devoted most of their time to their studies. This is only to be expected because University College at this time (from 1883 to 1908 to be precise) was run by the Jesuits who naturally insisted on high standards from their own men.

Frank kept his nose to the academic grindstone and graduated with an Honours BA in Classics in 1902.

Next came three years of philosophical studies in Chieri, near Turin in northern Italy. We know little about his years in Italy, except that during holidays he was free to travel around the country where he could stay, *gratis,* in Jesuit houses provided he did not stop over for more than three nights. He began to study Italian painting seriously and he photographed many masterpieces on a systematic basis. Florence was his favourite city, but Venice ran it a close second. While studying art in the galleries of these cities, he paid particular attention to the compositional skill of the Old Masters — an interest that would certainly be reflected later in his own photography. During his summer holidays there, he managed to photograph such exotic spots as the Lido of Venice and the Casino at Monte Carlo.

On his second return to Ireland, in September 1906, he taught for five years at Belvedere College, his old *alma mater* in Dublin. There he founded the college magazine and the camera club which still flourish. In 1909 he accompanied his uncle, the Bishop, on a voyage to Rome via Lisbon.

Since Frank's sister was a nun in the papal household, they were able to arrange to have breakfast with the Pope. Afterwards, Frank took a portrait of His Holiness (now Saint) Pius X.

ON THE s.s. TITANIC

In 1911 it was time to begin theological studies in Milltown Park, Dublin, where Frank was ordained a priest by his Uncle Robert in 1915. Before that, however, Uncle Robert was instrumental in providing his nephew with a memorable present: a first-class ticket for the first two stages of the maiden voyage of the *Titanic*. In April 1912, Frank sailed from Southampton to Cherbourg and from Cherbourg to Queenstown (now Cobh) in Ireland aboard that ill-fated liner.

An American family offered to pay his fare for the third leg of the *Titanic's* passage to New York. From the Marconi Room, Harold Bride sent a message to the Provincial Superior of the Jesuits in Dublin asking if Frank could stay on board. When they reached Cork harbour there was an answering message. It said, succinctly: 'GET OFF THAT SHIP — PROVINCIAL'.

In later years, he used to say that this was the only time that Holy Obedience had saved a man's life! Anyhow, off that ship he had to get. And from the tender at Queenstown he took the last extant photograph of Captain Smith — gazing, ironically, into a life-boat.

Among the many photographs he took during the voyage was one which shows a small boy whipping his spinning-top on the Saloon Deck, watched by his father and another passenger. Twenty-five years later, the *London Weekly Illustrated* would describe this as 'the most romantic photograph ever taken'. Let me explain why.

Early in April 1912, a rich Frenchman living near Nice decided to abscond with the family governess, taking his two sons, aged four and two, along with him. Hiring a car under an assumed name, he drove to Cherbourg, changed his name again (this time to Hoffman) and sailed on the *Titanic*. Frank Browne became friendly with the children during their first morning at sea. His photograph of the elder boy is captioned 'The Children's Playground'.

Both the father and the governess were lost in the catastrophe. The boys had been handed into one of the life-boats. They were rescued and taken to New York by the *Carpathia* and became known as 'the *Titanic* orphans'. Some weeks later, the boys' mother happened to see Frank Browne's photograph in a Spanish newspaper. Recognising her son, she travelled to New York where she was able to reclaim her children who were on the point of being adopted by Mrs Benjamin Guggenheim, the widow of one of the liner's victims.

His *Titanic* photographs include the only one ever taken of the ship's Marconi Room. On the days following the disaster, Browne photographs appeared on the front pages of newspapers around the world.

With the aid of glass slides, Frank put together an illustrated lecture on the *Titanic* which drew appreciative audiences. To his surprise this drew down the wrath of the White Star Line who wrote to him from Liverpool on 4 March 1913, asking that in any future lecture he refrain from any mention of the *Titanic* 'as we do not wish the memory of this calamity to be perpetuated'. Some hope.

IN THE TRENCHES: WORLD WAR I

In 1916 Frank Browne was appointed chaplain to the Irish Guards. His battalion was in the thick of World War I action in Flanders and the Somme. The non-combatant padre covered himself in glory, winning the M.C. and Bar and the *Titanic*. Field Marshal Lord Alexander of Tunis described him as 'the bravest man I ever met'. Injured five times and gassed once, the chaplain kept returning to the front and was a participant in 'The watch on the Rhine' in 1919.

For some interesting details of Father Browne's time as a chaplain, we are indebted to Prof Alfred O'Rahilly's life of William Doyle SJ, a colleague who died in the trenches. The two Jesuits served together on the Somme, at Locre, Wytschaete and Massines Ridge, at Ypres, Amiens and Arras. Father Browne first met up with his fellow Jesuit early in December 1916. O'Rahilly wrote:

Father Doyle gives a humorous description: 'Picture a good, respectable, deep, Irish ditch with plenty of water and mud in the bottom; scrape a fair-sized hole in the bank, cover the top with some sheets of iron, pile sandbags on top; and you have my dwelling. The door serves also as window and lets in not only light and air, but stray cats and rats galore and many creepy-crawly beasties, not to mention rain, snow and at times a breeze which must have been hatched at the North Pole.' It was in this dug-out that Fr. F.M. Browne S.J. met Fr. Doyle in December, 1916.

A subsequent chapter of O'Rahilly's book tells us that on 6 June 1917, at 11.50 pm, Fr Browne and Fr Doyle finally reached the little sandbag chapel which they had used when holding the line. There they lay down for an hour's rest on two stretchers borrowed from the huge pile waiting nearby for the morrow's bloody work. Leaving their servant fast asleep through sheer exhaustion, the two chaplains got up at 1 a.m. and prepared the altar. Fr. Doyle said Mass first and was served by Fr. Browne, who, not having yet made his Last Vows, renewed his Vows at the Mass, as he always did at home at Corpus Christi. It was surely a weird and solemn Renovation.

On 15 August 1917, the day before his comrade's death, Father Browne wrote again to his brother:

"Fr. Doyle is a marvel. You may talk of heroes and Saints, they are hardly in it! I went back the other day to see the old Dubs. as I heard they were having, we'll say, a taste of War. No one has yet been appointed to my place and Fr. Doyle has done double work. So unpleasant were the conditions that the men had to be relieved frequently. Fr. Doyle had nobody to relieve him and so he stuck to the mud and the shells, the gas and the terror."

This meeting took place on Wytschaete Ridge and there was, indeed, grim work to be done later that day. It was over a month later before the two men managed to get a break. Also on Wytschaete Ridge, Browne won his first Military Cross, accompanied by this citation:

He went forward with the battalion under very heavy fire and spent the whole day tending wounded and helping stretcher-bearers to find them under machine-gun fire. He showed splendid zeal and disregard for danger.

After the war had ended in November 1918, Father Browne advanced with the Irish Guards into Germany. He spent most of 1919 with them in Cologne and Bonn, taking many photographs during that year. In Wellington Barracks, London, the headquarters of the Irish Guards today, there is a magnificent album of his work entitled 'The Watch on the Rhine'. Embossed in gold letters on the morocco cover is the name, Major F.M. Browne, SJ, MC.

Father Browne with officers of the s.s. Port Melbourne, *the ship that brought him to Australia*

JOURNEY TO AUSTRALIA

When Father Browne returned to Dublin in 1920, he was appointed to serve in the city-centre Church of St. Francis Xavier. Records of his health are non-existent but one gathers that it began to fail him. Presumably his lungs were still affected by the 1918 gassing, mentioned above. Anyway it was for health reasons that he was sent on a voyage to Australia. Originally he was expected to return to his Dublin post in a matter of months. In fact it was November 1925 before he felt well enough to return home. The pictures in this book, therefore, are the work of a man in poor health. Not *that* sick, one might add: he was well enough to attend cricket matches in Brisbane and Adelaide, horse-racing in Melbourne and the sheep-shearing competitions at Kangaroobie!

Besides the Australian photographs themselves, the Browne Collection contains many pictures taken on the journeys to and from that country. He took portraits of the captain and various members of the crew of the s.s. *Port Melbourne* on the way out and of the s.s. *Orama* on the way back. He also photographed crewmen as they carried out their various duties such as testing the davits or serving beef-tea on the Saloon Deck. In great detail, he recorded the procedure involved in carrying out an oceanic survey, showing how a specially marked cask was prepared and dropped overboard at a strategic point in the Indian Ocean.

Father Browne sailed for Australia on 12 March 1924, leaving Falmouth on board the liner *Port Melbourne*. For the first week of the voyage, the sea was calm but his health was poor. He was thankful for the attention of the ship's doctor. As the weather warmed he began to feel better and enjoyed the remainder of the trip.

He stopped over for some weeks in Cape Town and took photographs all around the Cape Province of South Africa. While here he stayed with Fr John Morris who afterwards became the well-known editor of *The Southern Cross*. His photographs show a cross-section of the population ranging from children of all races playing together on the beach at Camps Bay to sophisticated adults admiring Watts' famous sculpture of 'Physical Energy' at Groote Schuur.

Continuing his journey to Australia on the *Arundel Castle*, Father Browne took dozens of pictures during the voyage, mostly showing the passengers at play and the members of the crew at work. When the ship arrived at Melbourne, he felt very much at home because he was met by a group of Irish Jesuits, several of whom had joined the Order on the same day as himself.

Australia must have been good for Fr Browne's health: he lived to the age of eighty. For thirty-five years after his return from Australia he was a member of the Mission Staff of the Irish Jesuits, giving parish missions and retreats throughout the four Home Countries.

The return journey to England began with a voyage on the *Orama* from Freemantle to Colombo, Ceylon, via the Cocos Islands. In Colombo he visited Kegalle School, run by the Irish Sisters of Mercy. At

Kandy he photographed the Temple of the Sacred Tooth and made an interesting portrait entitled 'Self in Rickshaw'. He also took an unusual photograph of himself beside an elephant.

From Ceylon he travelled via Somaliland and Yemen to Aden. Then, past Ethiopia, Sudan and Saudi Arabia, his ship sailed on through the Red Sea to Suez. Passing through that canal, he photographed life in Egypt on both the African and Asian banks before arriving in Port Said.

From Port Said he sailed across the Mediterranean Sea, first to Salonika in Greece and then, past Mount Etna on Sicily, to Naples. A three-day stopover there gave him the opportunity to visit Pompeii and photograph its extraordinary remains.

His next ship took him to Toulon in the south of France with its Napoleonic forts guarding the harbour; then to Gibraltar where again he stayed for three days. He took some fine pictures of the Rock itself and then crossed into Spain to visit Algeçiras and La Linea.

From Gibraltar he voyaged to Lisbon, which brought back memories of his 1909 visit, and from the Portuguese capital it was non-stop to Plymouth with a rough passage through the Bay of Biscay. After a short stay in England, Father Browne returned to Ireland.

Back home, Father Browne resumed his work at Gardiner Street Church in Dublin. Besides attending to his pastoral duties, it was at this stage that he began to photograph the city of Dublin in earnest: eventually he would accumulate nearly five thousand pictures of the capital. Another adventure:

he took lessons as a pilot in 1926. His Dublin photographs include many of the city and suburbs taken from the air. For the most part, the quality of these was poor — as he was the first to admit — but there are several excellent views of the city and of the Malahide area in north County Dublin.

Several hundred of these pictures went on exhibition in the Guinness Hop Store in Dublin during 1993. Guinness' Curator, Mr Peter Walsh, is on record as stating that this was the best attended exhibition he ever mounted. Later that year Wolfhound Press published *Father Browne's Dublin* which quickly became a best-seller.

Ever since his return from Australia, the photographer was active on another front: preparing for Ireland's first ever international Salon of Photography. This event duly took place in 1927 under the presidency of Sir John Lavery, R.A. The three vice-presidents were Hon. Mr Justice Hanna, K.C., General Eoin O'Duffy, Commissioner of the Irish Police and Father Browne who remained in office until 1939.

In 1926 Father Browne had joined the Irish Photographic Society and used to adjudicate competitions on its behalf. He contributed photographs to such magazines as *The Tatler and Sketch, Social and Personal* and *Irish Travel* (the fore-runner of *Ireland of the Welcomes*). Above all, he contributed monthly features on English cathedrals to The Kodak Magazine. In return, Kodak provided him with a free supply of film for life.

From 1931 to 1957, Father Browne was based in Emo, County Laois, in the midlands of Ireland. Then he was transferred to Milltown Park in Dublin where he had been ordained forty-two years earlier. His health was now deteriorating seriously and he had to undergo an operation in St. Vincent's Hospital. Ever the innovator, he set up his camera on tripod and time-hold so as to take an eerie self-portrait under anaesthetic in the operating-theatre.

Father Browne died in 1960. Knowing that he had taken more than 42,000 pictures during his lifetime, we are not surprised to learn that his Collection includes photographs of the Jesuit burial plot in Glasnevin cemetery where he himself now rests in peace.

Lord Alexander came to visit him on his death-bed and in The Irish Guards Association Journal, Lord Nugent wrote:

'Everyone in the Battalion, officer or man, Catholic or Protestant, loved and respected Father Browne and he had great influence for good. A great Christian, a brave and loveable man, we who knew him will always be grateful for his friendship and for the example that he set.'

PHOTOGRAPHER

Some readers will be interested in learning a little about the photographic equipment used by Father Browne before, during and after his Australian sojourn. Fortunately, his insurance policies have survived and from these we are able to trace the acquisitions he made during his long career. In the early days, from 1897 to 1916, he used a fairly primitive Kodak box camera. His first negatives were either postcard-sized or five inches square. Then he invested in a Contax I camera with a matching range-finder.

Before going to Australia he was given a present of a Plaubel Makina camera and a Zeiss lens. These were the German state-of-the-art technology of the time. He developed his own film. In Australia, on account of the heat, this was extremely difficult in the 1920s. To demonstrate just how difficult it was, he took a picture of two bottles of developing-chemicals cooling in wet towels on the verandah of a homestead in the outback.

When he returned from Australia, Father Browne graduated to a Contax II camera within months of its coming on the market. When 35mm photography was invented, he acquired one of the first 35mm cameras in Ireland, a Super Nettel (1931) which gave excellent definition. Eventually, in the late 1940s, he was given a present of a Leica camera which lasted him for the rest of his life.

After his death, Father Browne's negatives, all neatly annotated and dated, were put in a trunk which was stored in the Jesuit archives in Dublin. I discovered them there, quite by chance, twenty-five years later.

The bad news in 1985 was that the early photographs in the Collection, including all of the Australian ones, were on nitrate-based film that was beginning to deteriorate and would rapidly disintegrate. The task of transferring the images to safety film would cost many thousands of pounds. Fortunately sponsorship was secured — Allied Irish Bank and its assurance subsidiary, Ark Life, agreed to sponsor the restoration of the Collection. The

Irish Jesuits are most grateful to them for this praiseworthy undertaking. Similarly, I'm sure that readers of this book will be delighted that the Australian photographs have been saved for posterity.

Altogether, there are nearly nine hundred pictures of Australia in the Collection, all now saved. The conservation work was done by Mr David Davison, a member of the Irish Professional Conservators and Restorers Association, who has described Father Browne as 'one of the great photographic talents of this century.' Mr Davison, whose own work will be familiar to many Australian readers, expands on this assessment by commenting on the deeper element within these pictures:

> My initial excitement for Father Browne's photography was so intense that during the following weeks I found myself wondering whether I might have overreacted and that perhaps a more sober assessment was required. This reappraisal has continued for some years now during which time my son Edwin and I have made new negatives of the entire Collection and created a computerised database. This enhanced familiarity with the Collection has in fact confirmed my initial appraisal of the significance of this work. There is no other Collection of twentieth-century Irish photography of such stature, none so large, so wide in range of subject or rival in terms of artistic achievement. Father Browne's work is not just of significance for Ireland: I believe that as it becomes more widely known he will be acknowledged as one of the great photographers of the first half of this century.
>
> The skilful structure and timing of these photographs capture something of the experience of the moment. The pictures grip the imagination and convey atmosphere and mood and communicate feelings both pleasing and sometimes questioning. The viewer is challenged to engage in thought, to seek further meaning; surely at this point we are confronted with truly artistic expressive material.

Finally, I would like to thank Professor David Day of the Department of Modern History at University College, Dublin. As well as contributing the following portrait of Australia in Father Browne's time, he has been of enormous help in preparing captions for the photographs and has given me many insights into this continent that Father Browne photographed so diligently.

AUSTRALIA 1924-25

Professor David Day University College, Dublin

When Father Browne's ship steamed through the turbulent waters at the mouth of Port Phillip Bay in 1924, he was entering a far-flung British outpost whose people had been devastated by the recent Great War but which nevertheless looked to the future with brash confidence. It was a closeted society that was still groping towards an independent national identity less that twenty-five years after the federation of the former British colonies. It was a society in which the sectarian bitterness of the wartime conscription debates remained a live political issue. It was a society with an egalitarian ethos that co-existed with stark disparities of wealth and privilege. It was a society in which the British Protestant ascendancy was being eroded, both by an increasingly assertive

Catholic minority and a spreading scepticism. And this inchoate society occupied a continent the size of Europe, a land that had been settled by Europeans for less that 140 years and over which they were still striving to assert their moral and effective proprietorship.

Economically, and despite the high rate of urbanisation, Australia was still a mainly rural country in which features of the nineteenth century remained as reminders of the past. From the outback, horse-drawn drays still dragged the wealth of the interior - mainly wool - to seaboard cities where it was partly processed before being shipped to markets in Europe. Although Father Browne's photograph of the aptly-named Grand Hotel in Parkes (see page 53) does not have a sheep in sight, its decorative portico provides a sufficiently stark statement about the wealth that wool had brought to the otherwise rude interior.

Despite the wartime culling of its manhood, the 1920s were a period of optimism in Australia, a brave-faced optimism that was captured in a book of the time - *Australia Unlimited* - which suggested that Australia had the potential to emulate the United States, although most were determined that it should become a greater Britain in the south seas. The idea that Australia might develop to such a stage that it could wrest the leadership of the empire from a declining Britain was a persistent undercurrent to Australian thinking. Operating on such assumptions, an army of ex-servicemen and British migrants was encouraged to settle on plots of land carved out of the bush in order that they might till the thin and relatively infertile soil. In doing so, they continued the ongoing process of claiming the island continent by supplanting the original owners of the soil, the Aborigines.

Father Browne's photographs of the ordered fields of sugar cane and the splashing children at Manly Beach belied several underlying truths about white Australian society - that it was composed of a recently transplanted people, many of whom still referred to Britain as 'home'; that its steady dispossession of the Aborigines was continuing, with sporadic massacres on the far frontiers; and that it had as its core belief a 'white Australia' policy that tried to hold an increasingly hostile world at bay. Australia was conscious that its five million citizens were holding an island continent set in an ocean surrounded by populous and expansionist empires. Although it had helped the British empire to beat off the German challenge, it feared the prospect of before long having to face, possibly alone, a challenge from Japan. In the intervening period, it was determined that it should consolidate its hold on the continent.

Following the imperial slaughter of the first World War, Australia had redefined its identity, changing from 'white Australia' to 'British Australia'. Ethnicity became more important than race in defining who was to be kept out and who was to be allowed in. Many German Australians were deported after the war while new German immigrants were prevented from landing. Germanised towns in Australia had their names Anglicised. Although southern Europeans were still allowed entry, their numbers were severely restricted so that Australian society would remain at least 98% British. Irish nationalist tracts and songs were banned from import into Australia in order to protect the sanctity of the British empire upon which the safety of the Australian dominion largely depended. This was part of an increasingly rigid system of political and moral censorship that tried to blinker Australian eyes to changes that were taking place in the wider world. In a vain attempt to keep the blinker in place, a high import duty was imposed upon American films to protect the position of British culture and values in the Australian mind.

Australia was also concerned as to how it was perceived by the world. Films being exported from Australia were censored so that the wider world would have a positive image of the former convict colony. Newsreel footage of urban riots in Melbourne was seized and prevented from export; an American-financed feature film made in Australia about the country's convict days was subject to censorship to ensure that its audiences left cinemas with a favourable view of Australia. Even visitors such as Father Frank Browne were forced to submit their films for development and inspection by customs officials anxious to protect their country's reputation. The restriction remained in place until the rush of tourists for the 1956 Olympic Games in Melbourne forced its abandonment.

Despite the insecurities experienced by this supplanting society of British Australians, and the injustices perpetrated by them on the original Aboriginal occupiers and the non-Britishers who sought to emigrate there, it retained some of its earlier idealism. As a new society occupying a relatively under-developed continent, Australians believed they had an opportunity to construct a community that would be more wealthy, more egalitarian and more humane than the old, stratified European societies from which its people had sprung. And many found that the opportunities for wealth creation, and working conditions, the leisure possibilities and the relative 'openness' of Australian society answered their needs.

The fortuitous discovery of Father Browne's photographs provides us with a fresh window through which to witness the striving and glowing achievements of this predominantly British society while occasionally providing glimpses of a darker reality that shadowed the lives of its transplanted people.

Opposite page: The Quartermaster of s.s. *Port Melbourne*, Mr. J. McLeod, at the wheel

(above) Rev. W.P. Hackett SJ at Werribee College, Melbourne, with Mr and Mrs Egan and son. *(below)* An old colonial house at Geelong, Melbourne.

The Yarra River at Williamstown, near Melbourne, 1st May 1924.

(Opposite page)
Father Albert Power S.J., first Rector of
Victoria Diocesan Seminary, Melbourne,
with Mr Jacob (Manager) and Mrs Jacob.

(above)
Captain Kearney of s.s. *Port Melbourne* en
route from Melbourne to Sydney.

(below)
Ferry-boat, Sydney Harbour, heading off
from Circular Quay.

(above)
On the Rocks at Sydney Cove. A tourist attraction nowadays, the Rocks was a sleazy part of the city in 1924.

(below)
The city from the harbour. The Custom House is on the left with the tower of the Lands Department visible left of centre. Circular Quay is in the foreground, its cafés and tea-rooms overlooking the ferry-berths.

(left)
'The Apprentices' at Riverview, Sydney. Father Browne stayed at Riverview, now a prestigious Jesuit College.

(below)
The Zoo landing-stage at Sydney Harbour.

(left)
Panoramic view of Sydney Harbour from the top of the Astor.

(below)
View of the Harbour from Astor. Sydney Harbour Bridge now joins the promontory on the left to the North Shore (background). On the right is Bennelong Point where the Opera House now stands.

(above) Mark Foy's department-store;

(below left) 'Law' at Nielsen Park Wharf;

(below right) Harbour traffic at Milson's Point which is opposite the city centre. The famous bridge now crosses the channel on the right. The steamer is heading towards Darling Harbour.

The Bank of New South Wales.

(opposite)

On the Penrith Road: 'Some Smash!'

(top)
The North Shore ferry, *Kubu*.

(middle)
Enjoying the surf at Balmoral Beach.

(bottom)
The Diocesan Seminary overlooking
Manly Beach. The area is notable for
its wonderful Norfolk Pines.

Aboriginal children at Middle Harbour.

(above)
Car ferry at Middle Harbour.

(below)
An Aboriginal family at their home.

Megalong Street, Leura.

Ladies viewing the
waterfall at Leura.

(Opposite page)
The Mall, Leura.

Mount Solitary from Lynton.

(Opposite page)
The Falls at Leura.

(right)
Two-horse-power at Katoomba, then a favourite spot for honeymooning couples. The elegant carriage was probably designed for the comfort of such visitors.

(below)
Panoramic view of Katoomba from the convent.

(above)
The Postman on horseback
at Kanowna.

(left)
Mr Martin Flynn and friends
at The Nest.

(above)
A shady picnic spot, showing the kind of shelter still in use. The summer temperature here often soars above 100° Fahrenheit.

(opposite page)
'A Head for Heights' at Govett's Leap in the Blue Mountains.

(left)
The Cliff Walk overlooks a rich variety of evergreen trees.

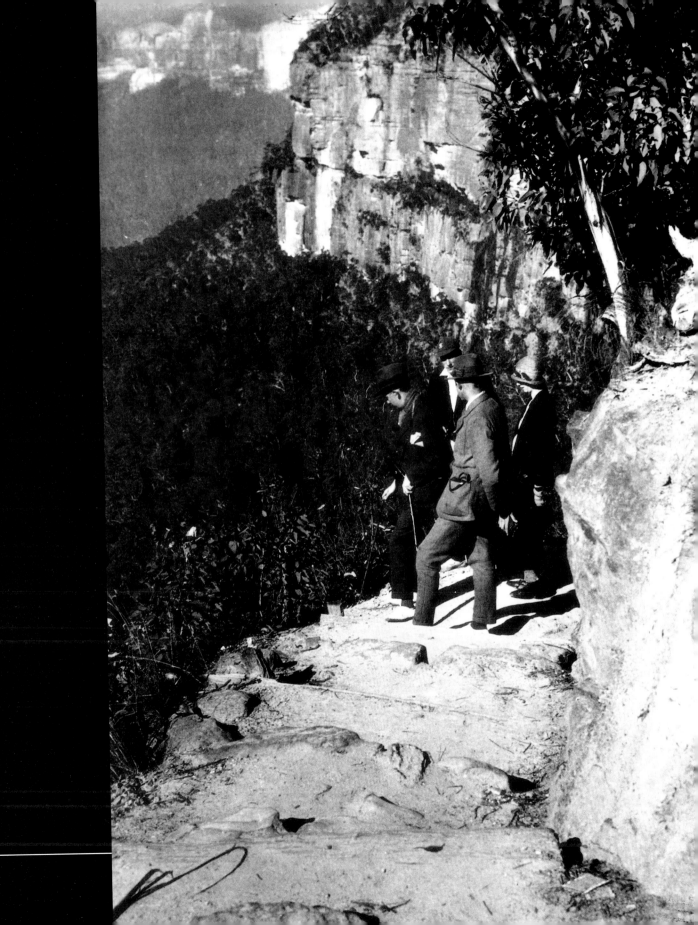

(left) A mountain home in the eucalyptus forest. Homesteads dotted this area and were at risk from forest fires. They still are.

(opposite page) Road-works at Mitchell's Pass, named after Major Mitchell, the Surveyor General of New South Wales in the 1830s.

(below) 'Rock Art' in a cave at the foot of the Blue Mountains. The photographer would have noticed some familiar surnames!

Photographic developer cooling on a verandah near Wollongong in the heat of an Australian noon.

(top left)
Enjoying the spray at Wollongong.

(top right)
At the boatyard, Wollongong.

(right)
Blackheath bus at Hat Hill. The emphasis on a strong shadow (in this instance of the photographer himself) is a device sometimes used by Fr Browne in his pictures.

(above)
Encampment at Hartley Vale.

(opposite page)
The Great Arch and Lake at Jenolan. The caves here attract thousands of visitors annually.

(below)
The Old Court House (1833) at Hartley Vale.

Erecting a water-tank at Newport. It would serve the building on the left which looks like a cottage hospital.

(above) Children on Narrabeen Beach, now a built-up resort north of Sydney.

(below) Where two seas almost meet. The woods above the isthmus give shelter to many distinguished holiday homes.

(above) Botany Bay, where Captain James Cook landed in 1770. This picture was taken from La Perouse, named after the French explorer who arrived here in 1788.

(opposite left) Boaters on the River Lachlan near Cowra. Lachlan Macquarie was Governor of New South Wales from 1809 to 1821.

(below) The Cronulla steam tram which ran from the nearby town of Cronulla to the coast at La Perouse.

(above)
Duntryleague House, exterior.
Duntryleague, named after the birthplace of James Dalton in Ireland, was built for him in 1876. The property was originally part of a 640-acre grant made to William Sampson in 1836. Benjamin Backhouse was the architect and R. Scott and J.J. McMurtrie were the stone masons. James Dalton left the house to his son, Patrick, a Jesuit priest. The Jesuits sold the property in the mid 1930s to the Orange Golf Club.

(left)
Hallway and staircase, Duntryleague House.
Duntryleague is a typical Squatter's home — which requires a word of explanation for non-Australian readers. 'Squatters' were the pioneers who pushed westwards beyond the Blue Mountains from the 1820s onwards. They acquired thousands of acres of sheep-grazing country, eventually becoming legally recognised as great land-owners. Many of them were among the richest families of New South Wales.

(right)
The Postman at Orange. The two houses in the background were very typical of the period.

(below)
Porch of Duntryleague House.

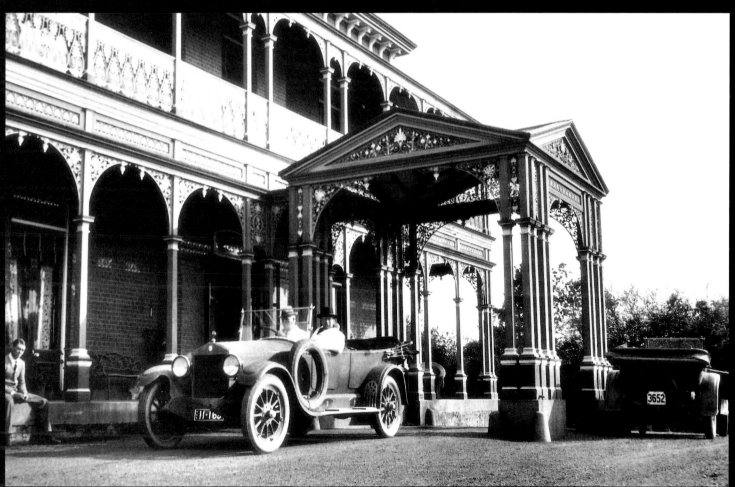

At the Horse Show and at the Prizegiving, Cudal.

(right)
The parlour car of the train at Toowoomba.

(below)
Summer Street, Orange.

(above)
The Shire Council of Conobles meets in the woods.

(opposite page)
(above) Father Browne with the Connolly family and friends.
(below) The Whitlock family 'berry-singing'.

(right) Goanna climbing tree. Note that the tree, like the others in the background, has been ring-barked to make it die.

(below) Bridge over the Bogan River near Tottenham.

Father Browne with a group of drovers near Gobabla.

(*above*) Main Street, Dubbo, a town built on the proceeds of sheep-farming. Note the width of the street to accommodate the passage of huge flocks and allow bullock drivers to manoeuvre their teams.

(*opposite page*) Hughie McLean's Exchange Hotel, Dubbo, and a 'mob' of sheep on the Kangaroobie road.

(above)
Wellington: the town *en fête*, probably for the celebration of Empire Day which went on to become Commonwealth Day.

(Opposite page)
Reflective lambs at Kangaroobie.

(above) The champion ram, Goliath, which sold for 3,000 guineas. It was only in 1966 that the Australian currency was changed to dollars.

(opposite page) (top left) Outdoor fleecing, using hand shears; *(bottom left)* Examining a fleece; *(right)* In the fleecing shed, using mechanical shears.

The gold-mine at Lucknow. Here we see a crushing-plant where the ore was extracted mechanically — an advance on the more primitive panning method used at Ophir Creek, overleaf.

Abandoned gold-mine at Ophir
Creek. A plaque on the monument
(left) marks the spot where 'payable'
gold was first found in Australia by
Edward Hargraves, John Lister,
James Tom and William Tom
between 7th and 12th April, 1851.

(left)
Gold was also found in Lewis Pond's Creek.

(bottom left)
Retreating from a bush fire.

(bottom right)
A trio of mules at full speed. Teams of bullocks were also used as draught-animals in this part of Australia at the time.

Canvas homes near Molong.

'Harvest Home' near Molong. (This photograph was brought by Mary Robinson, President of Ireland, as a gift on her state visit to Australia in 1992.)

(opposite page) Family group: the Murrays at their canvas home.

Ploughing with a team of seven horses in the wide country between Molong and Orange.

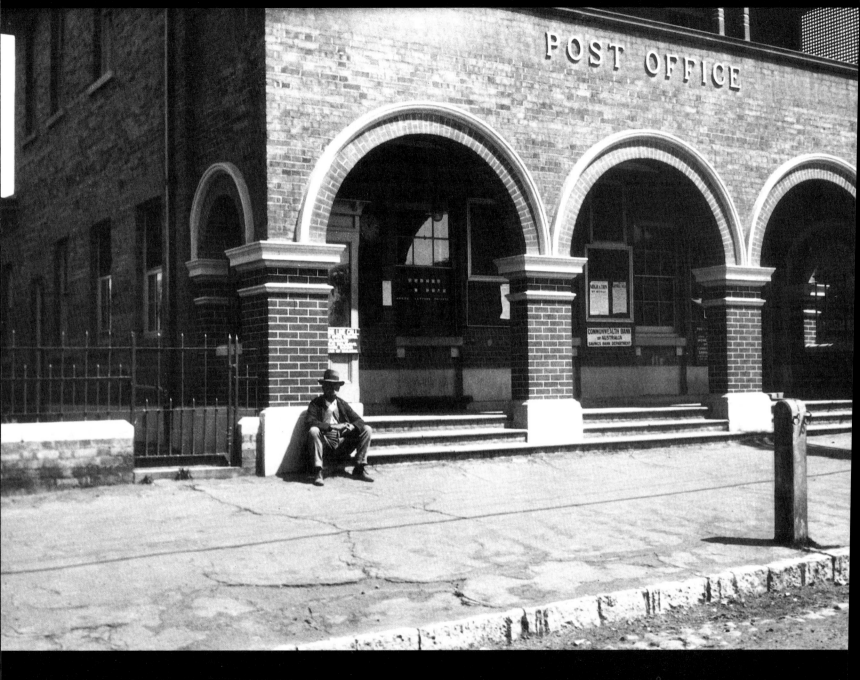

POST OFFICE

The Post Office at Molong. The Post Office was often the most impressive building in Australian towns and their most important employer. Throughout Australia, it had over 20,000 employees at this time.

Cyclist 'getting away from it all'
beyond Bathurst.

On the bowling-green at Bathurst.

Panoramic view of Carcoar.

Bush picnic near Carcoar
showing (left to right),
Mrs Corbett, Mrs Dalton,
Father Browne, Mick Dalton
and Bryan Dalton.

'Unlevel Crossing' in the outback near Ammerdown Run.
Note the dead trees in the background.

Split-rail advertising for
Dunn's Pharmacy.

(right) 'The Swagman' with his billy-can and bed-roll. Swagmen were itinerant workers, often highly skilled. Heavy borrowing in the 1920s led to a great depression during the 1930's when wool prices collapsed. 30% unemployment turned many townsmen into swagmen.

(below) The 'Humpy', an abandoned home where swagmen often spent the night.

The Sydney to Brisbane railway crossing the Parramatta River.

(above)
Railway-bridge from
Treasury Point, showing
South Brisbane across
the river.

(right)
Children at Gold Creek
School.

(opposite page)
At the Queensland Turf
Club, Ascot.

Great interest in the cricket scores outside the *Daily Mail* offices. The names of many of the firms seen here, such as the Camerons, are still prominent in Brisbane.

(opposite page)
Queensland versus an M.C.C. eleven at the Exhibition Ground, Brisbane. In 1928-9 this ground was used for Brisbane's first-ever Test Match. Subsequent Tests have been played at The Gabba.

Leaving Brisbane Quay: photograph
taken from deck of s.s. *Orama*.

(overleaf)

(above) Sunset from the boat deck of s.s. *Orama*
leaving Brisbane.

(below) Tug towing s.s. *Orama* from port of Brisbane.

Bathing at Sandgate, and the Pier.

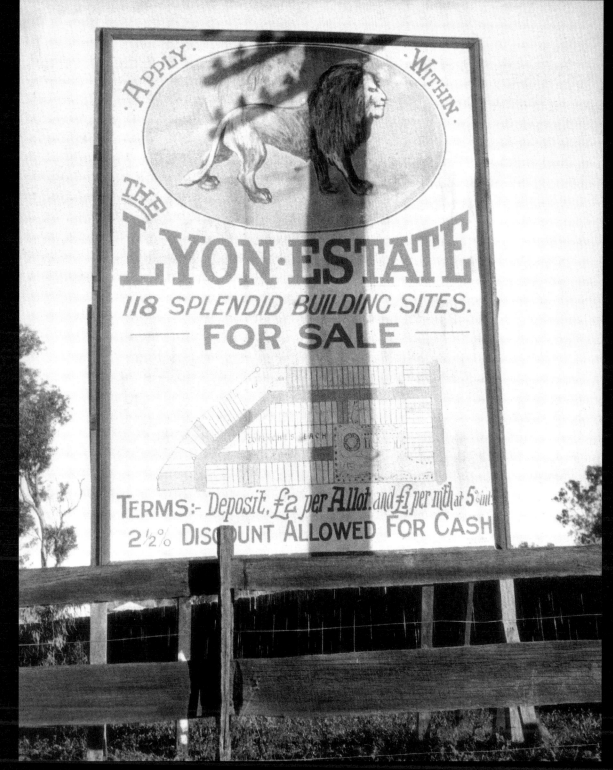

The Lyon Estate advertisement at Oxley. Besides the pre-inflation prices, the large size of the allotments is noteworthy.

The O'Carroll funeral at Oxley. Father Browne was obviously invited to take the photograph. The custom of women returning home after the Requiem and not attending the burial was common in Ireland until recent years.

(above) Christian Brothers' College, Mudgee.

(below) Ploughing in the pineapple fields of the Christian Brothers' College farm at Mudgee.

(above)
Pineapple close-up.

Railway Station at Landsborough, Queensland.

The Sugar Company yards at Morstone.
There were many factories like this
dotted around the sugar-growing area.

The sugar train

(opposite page) View from the train near Morstone. Narrow-gauge railways ran in a complicated network all around the sugar-growing fields.

The Maroochy River, Queensland, with Donethan's Rock in the background. The sugar-fields can be seen along both banks of the river.

(opposite page)

(above) Drawbridge on the Maroochy River. Raised to allow passage of Father Browne's ferry, it carried one of the narrow-gauge railways seen earlier.

(below) Ferry-boat and barge on the Maroochy River. The barge was for the long-distance transportation of sugar-cane. Donethan's Rock can be seen on the right.

(top left)
The Banana Plantation.

(top right)
Meat ants' nest.

(left)
Gates to the Archbishop's farm, St. Isadore's, near Mapleton.

(opposite page)

Sleeping quarters on the verandah, with mosquito-nets. To sleep out of doors like this is still a common practice in the summer months.

Rounding the bend: on the railway at Spring Bluffs.

(opposite page)

The railway-station at Murphy's Creek.

(*above*) The Mannix children, Donald and Evelyn, at the railway-station, Toowoomba.
(*right*) Father Colman and his car at Toowoomba.
(*below*) Margaret Street, Toowoomba, with the post office on the left.
(*opposite page*) Children of the Darling Downs.

Novices of the Sisters of Mercy from All Hallows Convent, Brisbane, photographed with Father Browne at Tamborine. The photographer himself is still moving *(centre)* having dashed in to take his seat leaving the camera on too short a time-release!

(opposite page) In the depths of the tropical forest, Queensland outback.

Driving through the tropical forest.

(opposite page) A shop in a clearing in the tropical forest.

QUEENSLAND

The Murray Mallee, South Australia, from Mount Lofty in the hills above Adelaide.

(left)
Heavy traffic on the Port Road leading from Adelaide city to Port Adelaide.

(below)
Test cricket for The Ashes: Australia v England at Adelaide. This was the ground where 'bodyline' bowling became infamous in 1932. St Peter's Cathedral in the background helps give Adelaide its appelation, 'The City of Spires'.

Overview of the port, Fremantle, Western Australia.

(opposite page) Panoramic view of Claremont, Western Australia, from Loreto Convent.

Panoramic view of Perth from the Municipal Gardens.
A modern concrete bridge now crosses the bay in the foreground.

(opposite page)

(above) Reflections on the Swan River, Perth.
(below) Making sand-castles on the banks of the Swan River at Como.

Crewman plumbing the depths off Fremantle breakwater.

(opposite page)
The s.s. *Orama* about to leave Australia.

'Australia, Fare thee Well!'